SEMA INSTITUTE OF YOGA

P.O.Box 570459
Miami, Florida, 33257
(305) 378-6253 Fax: (305) 378-6253

First U.S. edition 1997

© 1997 By Reginald Muata Ashby

The author is available for group lectures and individual counseling. For further information contact the publisher.

Ashby, Muata
The Parents Guide To The Ausarian Resurrection Myth: How to Teach Yourself and Your Child the Principles of Universal Mystical Religion.
ISBN: 1-884564-30-5

Library of Congress Cataloging in Publication Data

1 Parenting 2 Egyptian Philosophy, 3 Spiritual Studies.

Cruzian Mystic Books

Also by Muata Ashby

Egyptian Yoga: The Philosophy of Enlightenment
Initiation Into Egyptian Yoga: The Secrets of Sheti

For more listings see the back section.

For a complete listing of titles send for the free *Egyptian Yoga Catalog*

Attention parents: This manual has been designed for use with the children's book: *The Story of Asar, Aset and Heru.*

The Story of
Asar, Aset and Heru
An Ancient Egyptian Legend

Story book and Coloring book
by
Dr. Muata Abhaya Ashby

Author's Foreword

Who Were the Ancient Egyptians and What is Yoga Philosophy?

The Ancient Egyptian religion (*Shetaut Neter*), language and symbols provide the first "historical" record of Yoga Philosophy and Religious literature. Egyptian Yoga is what has been commonly referred to by Egyptologists as Egyptian "Religion" or "Mythology," but to think of it as just another set of stories or allegories about a long lost civilization is to completely miss the greatest secret of human existence. Yoga, in all of its forms and disciplines of spiritual development, was practiced in Egypt earlier than anywhere else in history. This unique perspective from the highest philosophical system which developed in Africa over seven thousand years ago provides a new way to look at life, religion, the discipline of psychology and the way to spiritual development leading to spiritual Enlightenment. Egyptian mythology, when understood as a system of Yoga (union of the individual soul with the Universal Soul or Supreme Consciousness), gives every individual insight into their own divine nature and also a deeper insight into all religions and Yoga systems.

Diodorus Siculus (Greek Historian) writes in the time of Augustus (first century B.C.):

"Now the Ethiopians, as historians relate, were the first of all men and the proofs of this statement, they say, are manifest. For that they did not come into their land as immigrants from abroad but were the natives of it and so justly bear the name of autochthones (sprung from the soil itself), is, they maintain, conceded by practically all men..."

"They also say that the Egyptians are colonists sent out by the Ethiopians, Osiris having been the leader of the colony. For, speaking generally, what is now Egypt, they maintain, was not land, but sea, when in the beginning the universe was being formed; afterwards, however, as the Nile during the times of its inundation carried down the mud from Ethiopia, land was gradually built up from the deposit...And the larger parts of the customs of the Egyptians are, they hold, Ethiopian, the colonists still preserving their ancient manners. For instance, the belief that their kings are Gods, the very special attention which they pay to their burials, and many other matters of a similar nature, are Ethiopian practices, while the shapes of their statues and the forms of their letters are Ethiopian; for of the two kinds of writing which the Egyptians have, that which is known as popular (demotic) *is learned by everyone, while that which is called sacred* (hieratic), *is understood only by the priests of the Egyptians, who learnt it from their Fathers as one of the things which are not divulged, but among the Ethiopians, everyone uses these forms of letters. Furthermore, the orders of the priests, they maintain, have much the same position among both peoples; for all are clean who are engaged in the service of the gods, keeping themselves shaven, like the Ethiopian priests, and having the same dress and form of staff, which is shaped like a plough and is carried by their kings who wear high felt hats which end in a knob in the top and are circled by the serpents which they call asps; and this symbol appears to carry the thought that it will be the lot who shall dare to attack the king to encounter death-carrying stings. Many other things are told by them concerning their own antiquity and the colony which they sent out that became the Egyptians, but about this there is no special need of our writing anything."*

The Ancient Egyptian texts state:

"Our people originated at the base of the mountain of the Moon, at the origin of the Nile river."

◢◣◥◤

"KMT"
"Egypt," "Burnt," "Land of Blackness,""Land of the Burnt People."

KMT (Ancient Egypt) is situated close to Lake Victoria in present day Afrika. This is the same location where the earliest human remains have been found, in the land currently known as Ethiopia-Tanzania. Recent genetic technology as reported in the new encyclopedias and leading news publications has revealed that all peoples of the world originated in Afrika and migrated to other parts of the world prior to the last Ice Age 40,000 years ago. Therefore, as of this time, genetic testing has revealed that all humans are alike. The earliest bone fossils which have been found in many parts of the world were those of the African Grimaldi type. During the Ice Age, it was not possible to communicate or to migrate. Those trapped in specific locations were subject to the regional forces of weather and climate. Less warmer climates required less body pigment, thereby producing lighter pigmented people who now differed from their dark-skinned ancestors. After the Ice Age when travel was possible, these light-skinned people who had lived in the northern, colder regions of harsh weather during the Ice Age period moved back to the warmer climates of their ancestors, and mixed with the people there who had remained dark-skinned, thereby producing the Semitic colored people. "Semite" means mixture of skin color shades.

Therefore, there is only one human race who, due to different climactic and regional exposure, changed to a point where there seemed to be different "types"of people. Differences were noted with respect to skin color, hair texture, customs, languages, and with respect to the essential nature (psychological and emotional makeup) due to the experiences each group had to face and overcome in order to survive.

From a philosophical standpoint, the question as to the origin of humanity is redundant when it is understood that _ALL_ come from one origin which some choose to call the "Big Bang" and others "The Supreme Being."

> **"Thou makest the color of the skin of one race**
> **to be different from that of another, but**
> **however many may be the varieties of**
> **mankind, it is thou that makes them all to**
> **live."**
>
> Ancient Egyptian Proverb from *The Hymns of*
> *Amun*

Historical evidence proves that Ethiopia-Nubia already had Kingdoms at least 300 years before the first Kingdom-Pharaoh of Egypt.

> *"Ancient Egypt was a colony of Nubia -*
> *Ethiopia. ...Osiris having been the leader of the*
> *colony..."*
>
> *"And upon his return to Greece, they gathered*
> *around and asked, "tell us about this great land*
> *of the Blacks called Ethiopia." And Herodotus*
> *said, "There are two great Ethiopian nations,*
> *one in Sind (India) and the other in Egypt."*
>
> **Recorded by Egyptian high priest *Manetho* (300 B.C.)**
> **also Recorded by *Diodorus* (Greek historian 100 B.C.)**

The pyramids themselves however, cannot be dated, but indications are that they existed far back in antiquity. The Pyramid Texts (hieroglyphics inscribed on pyramid walls) and Coffin Texts (hieroglyphics inscribed on coffins) speak authoritatively on the constitution of the human spirit, the vital Life Force along the human spinal cord (known in India as *"Kundalini"*), the immortality of the soul, reincarnation and the law of Cause and Effect (known in India as the Law of Karma).

What is Yoga Philosophy and Spiritual Practice

Since a complete treatise on the theory and practice of yoga would require several volumes, only a basic outline will be given here.

When we look out upon the world, we are often baffled by the multiplicity which constitutes the human experience. What do we really know about this experience? Many scientific disciplines have developed over the last two hundred years for the purpose of discovering the mysteries of nature, but this search has only engendered new questions about the nature of existence. Yoga is a discipline or way of life designed to promote the physical, mental and spiritual development of the human being. It leads a person to discover the answers to the most important questions of life such as Who am I?, Why am I here? and Where am I going?

The literal meaning of the word YOGA is to *"YOKE"* or to *"LINK"* back. The implication is: to link back to the original source, the original essence, that which transcends all mental and intellectual attempts at comprehension, but which is the essential nature of everything in CREATION. While in the strict or dogmatic sense, Yoga philosophy and practice is a separate discipline from religion, yoga and religion have been linked at many points throughout history. In a manner of speaking, Yoga as a discipline may be seen as a non-sectarian transpersonal science or practice to promote spiritual development and harmony of mind and body thorough mental and physical disciplines including meditation, psycho-physical exercises, and performing action with the correct attitude.

The disciplines of Yoga fall under five major categories. These are: *Yoga of Wisdom, Yoga of Devotional Love, Yoga of Meditation, Tantric Yoga* and *Yoga of Selfless Action.* Within these categories there are subsidiary forms which are part of the main disciplines. The important point to remember is that all aspects of yoga can and should be used in an integral fashion to effect an efficient and harmonized spiritual movement in the practitioner. Therefore, while there may be an area of special emphasis, other elements are bound to become part of the yoga program as needed. For example, while a yogin may place emphasis on the yoga of wisdom, they may also practice devotional yoga and meditation yoga along with the wisdom studies.

While it is true that yogic practices may be found in religion, strictly speaking, yoga is neither a religion or a philosophy. It should be thought of more as a way of life or discipline for promoting greater fullness and experience of life. Yoga was developed at the dawn of history by those who wanted more out of life. These special men and women wanted to discover the true origins of creation and of themselves. Therefore, they set out to explore the vast reaches of consciousness within themselves. They are sometimes referred to as "Seers," "Sages," etc. Awareness or consciousness can only be increased when the mind is in a state of peace and harmony. Thus, the disciplines of meditation (which are part of Yoga), and wisdom (the philosophical teachings for understanding reality as it is) are the primary means to controlling the mind and allowing the individual to mature psychologically and spiritually.

The teachings which were practiced in the Ancient Egyptian temples were the same ones later intellectually defined into a literary form by the Indian Sages of Vedanta and Yoga. This was discussed in my book *Egyptian Yoga: The Philosophy of Enlightenment.* The Indian Mysteries of Yoga and Vedanta represent an unfolding and intellectual exposition of the Egyptian Mysteries. Also, the study of Gnostic Christianity or Christianity before Roman Catholicism will be useful to our study since Christianity originated in Ancient Egypt and was also based on the Ancient Egyptian Mysteries. Therefore, the study of the Egyptian Mysteries, early Christianity and Indian Vedanta-Yoga will provide the most comprehensive teaching on how to practice the disciplines of yoga leading to the attainment of Enlightenment.

The question is how to accomplish these seemingly impossible tasks? How to transform yourself and realize the deepest mysteries of existence? How to discover "who am I?" This is the mission of Yoga Philosophy and the purpose of yogic practices. Yoga does not seek to convert or impose religious beliefs on any one. Ancient Egypt was the source of civilization and the source of religion and Yoga. Therefore, all systems of mystical spirituality can coexist harmoniously within these teachings when they are correctly understood.

The goal of yoga is to promote integration of the mind-body-spirit complex in order to produce optimal health of the human being. This is accomplished through mental and physical exercises which promote the free flow of spiritual energy by reducing mental complexes caused by ignorance. There are two roads which human beings can follow, one of wisdom and the other of ignorance. The path of the masses is generally the path of ignorance which leads them into negative situations, thoughts and deeds. These in turn lead to ill health and sorrow in life. The other road is based on wisdom and it leads to health, true happiness and enlightenment.

Our mission is to extol the wisdom of yoga and mystical spirituality from the Ancient Egyptian perspective and to show the practice of the teachings through our books, videos and audio productions. You may find a complete listing of other books by the author, in the back of this volume.

INTRODUCTION

Many people look on the world and see the troubles of violence, crime, the eroding values of society and other ills of humanity as an inevitable movement towards disaster. It is certainly possible for society to lead itself to ruin. This has happened in the past. However, is this inevitable and if not how can it be averted? Human life has a definite purpose and the organization of humanity into societies and civilizations is in reality supposed to further the goals of humanity and not be a source or venue for experiencing negativity and suffering.

The spiritual texts from all religious traditions from around the world affirm that every human being comes from a divine source and is destined to once again discover his or her divine essence. But is this true and if so how is this possible? Some people simply believe that you can have faith in a God and that that alone will save you but is that enough?

Some people believe that there is a God who created humanity and the universe. These people are called *theists*. Others believe that there is no God and that Creation occurred by chance. It just exists, coming from nowhere and going nowhere. These people are known as *atheists*. The theists rely on faith while the atheists say that nothing outside of what the senses can perceive is real, and that anything that is perceived outside of the senses represents imagination or insanity. The *agnostic* believes that there can be no proof of the existence of God but does not deny the possibility that God exists. The *gnostic* (Ancient Egyptians, Hindus, Buddhists, and others who practiced Yoga and Mystical Spirituality before and during the early Christian era), on the other hand believes that there is a spiritual basis for all existence and that this essence can be discovered and experienced. It must be clearly understood that the spiritual essence of a human being as well as the spiritual essence of the universe cannot be discovered by a person who believes that they do not exists because the belief itself is a constricting element which blocks the perception of anything that does not fall within its framework of understanding. Likewise the mind has such creative power that a person can convince themselves of something that is not real. Therefore, how can spiritual experience be said to exist? True spiritual experience requires a scientific mystical movement towards understanding and then transcending it. Then the concepts of existence and non-existence are transcended and it is then that God, who is transcendental of all, can be discovered. Therefore, strong belief in a religious dogma or philosophy as well as the disbelief in spiritual reality are both forms of obstruction to real spiritual evolution.

Another teaching is that of *reincarnation* and *transmigration* of the soul. If you do not believe that there is a greater power controlling the universe then you must believe that the earth has no origin or purpose, that it is just here and that it popped out of nowhere. This goes for humanity as well. If you believe that your likes and dislikes, your abilities and your psychological makeup are just by chance then you must believe that life is a random, arbitrary, capricious or whimsical expression of nature or the cosmic joke of some alien race which looks down on human beings as human beings look down on rodents. However, logic tells us that something cannot come from something that is not existent and real. Also, logic tells us that if there is no reincarnation then all of the achievements of a person's life are meaningless and worthless. Some people base their life on this premise and so they seek to live life for three purposes, to experience sensual pleasures, acquire wealth and to leave it for their progeny. They die a pathetic death, not having discovered a deeper meaning of life, only to see their possessions, which they worked so hard for, going to others who are undeserving and equally greedy and callous. The teachings of reincarnation speak of an orderly journey of the soul through various embodiments wherein it meets other souls and through their interaction spiritual growth is made possible. In modern times para-psychological studies have proven that reincarnation does occur as the ancient scriptures always said.

So what is Creation and what is the purpose of life? The ancients discovered that Creation is in essence the mind of God and that all life within Creation is essentially an emanation or ray of divine consciousness just as a ray of sunshine is an emanation of the sun. However, what would happen if the ray of sunshine were to forget that it came from the sun? It would get lost in the universe and wander throughout the vastness of Creation. In the same way the soul becomes involved in various situations and find itself associated with countless forms of existence just as a sunray can encounter many conditions as it reflects in many different surfaces (glass, water, etc.). It would need some way to discover its true identity, its true origin. This is the journey of the human soul, to end its wandering in the wilderness of human existence and to discover its true identity as divine, immortal, supremely blissful and content. How is this exalted view of life to be experienced? This is the true purpose of mystical religion and yoga philosophy.

Think of your dream world. The ancient Sages studied the human mind and discovered that it is not just a simple mechanism by which people can have an awareness of the world through the sense organs but that it has an unimaginable depth like an ocean below the waves. When you dream you create your own universe and you become the main character in that universe. In the same manner if you were able to go deeper within yourself in a conscious and disciplined way you would discover that your physical life is also a kind of dream which you have created and that you are the main character of that as well. It is a longer dream as opposed to when you sleep at night but nevertheless it is the same kind of experience. The difference in length between ordinary life and a dream is a divinely ordained feature of Creation which allows a human being time to study and reflect upon his or her condition and to take the necessary actions to gain wisdom in order to discover his or her true identity.

The course of one's spiritual evolution (journey of self-discovery) is not something that can be entrusted to "others." You cannot say that television or the church or the government or the school should teach your child and then expect that society will become a better place. You are the one who is responsible for humanity and if you do not accept your responsibility you are not upholding the teachings and the true spirit of religion. You cannot hold this kind of attitude and then wonder why the world is in the state that it is. All you need to do to uphold righteousness is to live up to the needs of your own conscience. Seek to fulfill the deeper needs of your own soul and never compromise your conscience by accepting what is unrighteous, unjust and selfish. Become introspective. Seek to discover what is true and good and then seek to share your wealth with others and to help others to discover their inner gifts. This is the way to practice universal religion and yoga philosophy.

HOW TO TEACH YOUR CHILD THE PRINCIPLES OF UNIVERSAL RELIGION AND YOGA

"An infant's Soul is altogether a thing of beauty to see, not yet befouled by body's passions, still all but hanging from the Cosmic Soul! But when the body grows in bulk and draweth down the Soul into it's mass, then does the Soul cut off itself and bring upon itself forgetfulness, and no more shares in the Beautiful and Good (God); and this forgetfulness becometh vice."

Ancient Egyptian Proverb

Who am I, what am I doing here, why am I here, where am I going, is this all there is, what is creation and who created it, is there a god or goddess who created the universe and if so what is our relationship to him or her?. These are some of the most important questions in everyone's life. Human beings from the beginning of time have sought to explain or answer these questions in various ways. Some simply seek to live their life trying to achieve as much happiness as they can while they live, not worrying about the deeper implications of life while others seek desperately for an answer to these haunting issues.

In ancient times, once civilization rose to a state wherein

people had sufficient time away from the concerns of food and shelter, the possibility arose in which the inquiring mind of a human being could be exercised. This was the dawn of mystical philosophy or the study of the mystical origins of creation and of humanity. Those who were able to spend their time investigating creation were called Sages and as they inquired into the nature of their own being through reflectiveness and meditation and they discovered the wonder of life and the deeper essence of Creation. They set out to explain what they discovered to the rest of humanity but knowing that this explanation requires intellectual and emotional maturity they created stories and legends which contain many levels of teaching for those who are novices as well as for those who are advanced in their understanding. These stories came to be known as *Myths* and *Parables*. These myths and parables form the basis of what is generally referred to as *Religion* and *Yoga*.

A myth is a message which uses the vehicle of ordinary and sometimes supernatural events and characters in order to impart certain teachings about the nature of creation and the origins and destiny of a human being. Since a myth is not necessarily a story about something factual it is not bound by the need for historical accuracy or factual accounts. Rather, a myth contains a deeper level of reality with respect to the principles of life and the way in which the Divine manifests in, through and as nature and as human life.

So now with this understanding about myths we need to find out what religion is. The term religion comes from the Latin word *"Relegare"* which uses the word roots *"RE"*, which means *"BACK"*, and *"LIGON"*, which means *"to hold, to link, to bind."* Therefore, the essence of true religion is that of linking back, specifically, linking the souls of its followers back to their original source and innermost essence, God. In this sense the terms "religion" and "yoga" are synonymous. This "source," which is the underlying reality behind every object in Creation, is described as unborn, undying, eternal and immortal, and is known by an endless number of names, some of which are:

Consciousness, Self, Higher Self, God, Goddess, Supreme Being, Divine Self, Eternal Self, Soul, Pure Consciousness, Brahman, All, Allah, Jehovah, Neter Neteru, Creator, Absolute, Heavenly Father, Divine Mother, Great Spirit. These various names, while arising from various traditions and separate cultures, in reality represent the same divine and transcendental principle.

Ancient Egypt was the first culture to "create" religion and to bring it to its quintessential form. Its impact was so strong that Ancient Egyptian Religion (Shetaut Neter) has had an effect on modern day religions (See the book *Egyptian Yoga: The Philosophy of Enlightenment*). In ancient times myth was a part of every human endeavor, be it the legal profession, the healing profession or the government. They recognized that myth and religion are not just optional concerns of life but the very heart of life, the very center of that which gives life meaning and that which leads a human being to discover what is god, true and beautiful in life. In order for this to be possible, a community or society must be disposed to uphold the universal principles of religion and spiritual evolution and secondly, the leaders (government leaders, parents, teachers and all others who work in a society) must see themselves as an integral part of society and not as replaceable parts of a machine. Every spec in Creation is here for a reason and every member of society has an effect on society.

A Spiritual Preceptor or Sage is someone who can understand and properly explain the teachings contained in the myth for various levels of personalities is a most important member of society because if spiritual truths are not understood and upheld by society there will be chaos, greed and violence in the community. A Sage is someone who has advanced on the spiritual path and this means that he or she has made strides towards conquering anger, hatred, greed, lust, egoistic desires and selfishness. Such a person is the benefactor of society and the living source of goodwill and spiritual wisdom for society. It does not matter how much technical advancement and wealth you have if you live a life of unrest and inner discontent. A spiritual preceptor is not just a person who preaches and encourages others to "have faith" and to "be good" but someone who lives and breaths the teachings and can lead another person to achieve the highest spiritual realization. This is also why the elders of a community are to be revered and treated as leaders. Their life experience has given them the opportunity to gather wisdom and insight into the folly of materialism and atheism.

A human being is a complex individual. There are many facets to the human personality and the most important of these is the soul. Using religious terminology, the soul is the source of the individual human being. This soul has incarnated on earth into human form in order to gain certain experiences. These experiences will lead it to discover its true origin and destiny and this ideal is the very heart of the Ausarian Resurrection Myth of Ancient Egypt.

The Ausarian Resurrection Myth centers around the character of the king Asar or Osiris. Asar is the son of Ra, the Supreme Being and Creator of the Universe who emerges out of the primeval waters of unformed matter. Asar was a virtuous leader who established civilization and the knowledge of God (religion) throughout the world. Asar was killed by his brother out of greed and jealousy. Asar was brought back to life by Aset (Isis) and then they beget a child, Heru (Horus), who will re-establish righteousness on earth by meeting the challenge of his Uncle, Set, who has unrighteously usurped the throne of Ancient Egypt.

The story of a savior who is persecuted at birth and who will grow to re-establish righteousness and the way to practice true religion occurs in Christianity in the form of Jesus and in Hinduism in the form of the god Krishna who was, like Horus, persecuted by his own uncle.

Have you heard a similar story to this one in recent times? Two of the most important movies of modern times contain exactly the same formula. The *Star Wars* movie series is an example of the impact of this story. Also the movie *Lion King* is a clear example of the formula which was presented over seven thousand years ago in Ancient Egypt. If this is the case would it not be a worthwhile endeavor to re-examine the teachings of the Ausarian Resurrection Myth? What is it about this theme which strikes at the very heart of human sentiment?

> "If you are wise, train children to be pleasing to God. If they are straight and take after you, take good care of them. Do everything that is good for them. They are your children, your KA begot them. Don't withdraw your heart from them. But an offspring can make trouble. If they stray and neglect your council and disobey all that is said, with mouth spouting evil speech, then punish them for all their talk. God will hate them who cross you. Their guilt was determined in the womb. Those who God makes boatless cannot cross the water."
>
> Ancient Egyptian Proverb

When children are born they need guidance and a solid foundation. If these are not received by parents directly then it falls on the community and in a greater sense the society to look after their physical, mental and spiritual wellbeing. However, what if society develops in a manner which promotes materialism and the idea of the separation of church and state or the idea that religion is false and a waste of time? What happens if society develops the ideal of fame and fortune above spiritual enlightenment and inner peace? If this happens the result will be a litigious society wherein many people are out to satisfy their own greed and selfish desires, a community wherein people have lost a sense of community values leading to a situation wherein people fend for themselves and live at the expense of others.

When this occurs people who are not looked after (children) may develop the negative traits of their personalities and this will lead to all the forms of crime and violence which can plague a society and lead to its ruin. When a child grows up believing that he or she has no connection to nature and to a higher power

their despair, anger, hatred and greed take over the mind and
their is a development of dullness, ignorance and negativity in
the mind.

Spiritual ignorance develops in a human being when their is
no deeper spiritual awareness beyond the superficialities of life.
Spiritual Ignorance is termed as the absence of the knowledge of
the Higher Self. Dullness is the intensification of the negative
qualities of the mind. The degraded mental capacity manifests in
the forms of selfishness, greed, hatred, anger, lust and other
human failings. Anger and hatred lead to violence and self-
destruction.

> "The Soul that hath no knowledge of the
> things that are or knowledge of their nature, is
> blinded by the body's passions and tossed about.
> The wretched Soul, not knowing what it is,
> becomes the slave of bodies of strange form in
> sorry plight, bearing the body as a load; not as the
> ruler but as the ruled."
>
> Ancient Egyptian Proverb

All human beings are born with an innate desire. This is a
divinely ordained law. Desire exists in a human being because
the deeper spiritual essence of a human being, the soul, needs to
discover its deeper self, to dispel the ignorance in order to enter
into a higher plane of peace and inner fulfillment. If there were
no desire a human being would remain in a perpetual state of
dullness and insipidness. So desire is the very essence of life.
However, when there is ignorance about life in the mind a
human being enters into a process of negative desiring which is
oftentimes backed up by the society. The idea develops that
desiring pleasure and the accumulation of objects are the way to
fulfill life's desires. Desire is seen as the purpose of life and then
the meaning of life becomes equated with sense pleasures,
wealth, fame and name. The small amounts of satisfaction which
are felt after fulfilling a desire lead a person to believe that if they
fulfill all desires then there will be perpetual happiness. In reality
the fulfillment of a desire leads to the emergence of another in an
endless cycle.

Thus, out of ignorance and through lack of guidance a human being begins to seek for fulfillment in the experiences and objects of the world and since he or she cannot have everything that is desired at any given time disappointment, anger and hatred arise in the heart. If this anger is checked and sublimated, through growth in reason and inner spiritual awareness by understanding the error of desiring, a person can discover that what they desire is in reality something which worldly objects and worldly situations cannot give. Worldly situations and the attainment of worldly objects are only means to an end and not ends in themselves. However, if this factor is not understood and if a higher perspective of life is not achieved a human being hardens in their anger and violence and this is the source of the willingness to hurt others and oneself. In this manner desire becomes a great burden for a human being as well as for society. In reality a human being desires to know him/her Self and to discover supreme peace and happiness but this is only possible when their is knowledge of the Higher Self, as well as the absence of mental agitation and the delusion which comes from desiring objects of the world. A human being cannot give up desires altogether but he or she can learn to desire what is good and true through a process of developing every aspect of their personality.

> "Thou, alone can speak. Wonder at this glorious prerogative; and pay to the Supreme who gave to you the gift of life a rational and welcome praise, teaching your children wisdom, instructing the offspring of your loins in piety."
> -Ancient Egyptian Proverb

Children need to have a solid foundation with which they can relate to their fellow human beings, with nature and with God, the Self or Higher Power. Otherwise they enter into a process which begins with disintegration of their personality and which moves into a condition of self-destruction which may manifest as the consumption of negative thoughts, foods and substances that will promote unrest and dullness of mind. This may progress to violent behavior and sociopathic as well as suicidal tendencies. This is the ultimate degradation and humiliation of the soul.

All people, but children in particular, need to have a story of their own, something they can believe in and something which inspires them to greatness and exaltation. Their myth needs to inspire security and purpose while promoting inner peace and a sense of spiritual identity, that is, a sense of relationship with that which transcends ordinary human existence. In short, they need a sublime vision of life.

Children should be told early on that they have a soul and that they have a great purpose in life, that being to discover God in all things and to spread joy throughout the world. Once a child is well established in the spiritual philosophy, by being aquatinted with the general themes of their myth, it will be easier for them to develop an interest in the deeper mystical implications when they grow up. This is true even if they grow up and seem to go in a different direction. The spiritual basis of their youth will provide them with a basis to study and understand the deeper mystical teachings of any religion or yoga philosophy they may choose later in life. Is there any better legacy to pass down to them? The gift of spiritual wisdom is the greatest gift because without spiritual awareness all of the riches of the universe are useless and meaningless since life ultimately leads to death and letting go of all possessions. However, in order to acquire wisdom there must be a basis of mental and physical purity. As a parent you are in a uniquely advantageous position to manage the activities and associations of your child so as to lead them to opportunities wherein they can develop purity of heart (maakheru), meaning a healthy attitude towards spirituality and a sense of purpose in life.

WHAT IS YOGA?

What is Yoga? The literal meaning of the word YOGA is to *"YOKE"* or to *"LINK"* back. The implication is to link back individual consciousness to its original source, the original essence: Universal Consciousness. In a broad sense Yoga is any process which helps one to achieve liberation or freedom from the bondage to human pain and spiritual ignorance. So whenever you engage in any activity with the goal of promoting the discovery of your true Self, be it studying the wisdom teachings, exercise, fasting, meditation, breath control, rituals, chanting, prayer, etc., you are practicing yoga. If the goal is to help you to discover your essential nature as one with God or the Supreme Being or Consciousness, then it is Yoga. Yoga, in all of its forms as the disciplines of spiritual development, as practiced in Ancient Egypt earlier than anywhere else in history. The ancient scriptures describe how Asar, the first mythical king of Ancient Egypt, traveled throughout Asia and Europe establishing civilization and the practice of religion. This partially explains why the teachings of mystical spirituality known as Yoga and Vedanta in India are so similar to the teachings of Shetaut Neter (Ancient Egyptian religion - Egyptian Yoga). This unique perspective from the highest philosophical system which developed in Africa over seven thousand years ago provides a new way to look at life, religion, psychology and the way to spiritual development leading to spiritual Enlightenment. So Egyptian Yoga is not merely a philosophy but a discipline for promoting spiritual evolution in a human being, allowing him or her to discover the ultimate truth, supreme peace and utmost joy which lies within the human heart.

THE DEVELOPMENT OF HUMAN PERSONALITY

The personality of every human being is somewhat different from every other. However, the Sages of Yoga have identified four basic factors which are common to all human personalities. These factors are: **Emotion, Reason, Action and Will**. This means that in order for a human being to evolve, all aspects of the personality must progress in an integral fashion. Therefore, four major forms of Yoga disciplines have evolved and each is specifically designed to promote a positive movement in one of the areas of personality. The Yoga of Devotional Love enhances and harnesses the emotional aspect in a human personality and directs it towards the Higher Self. The Yoga of Wisdom enhances and harnesses the reasoning aspect in a human personality and directs it towards the Higher Self. The Yoga of Action enhances and harnesses the movement and behavior aspect in a human personality and directs it towards the Higher Self. The Yoga of Meditation enhances and harnesses the willing aspect in a human personality and directs it towards the Higher Self.

Religion uses all of the disciplines of yoga as a person aspires, purifies him or her self and discovers their higher nature. Thus, it would be beneficial for you to study the disciplines of yoga in all their forms in order to enhance your religious practice. *Egyptian Yoga* is a revolutionary new way to understand and practice Ancient Egyptian Mysticism, the Ancient Egyptian mystical religion (*Shetaut Neter*). The Egyptian Yoga Book Series shows how the Sages of ancient Africa created an intricate system for spiritual development which was incorporated in the religious system of Kamut (Ancient Egypt). This system of spiritual development was the object of study for all other civilizations of the ancient world. This included the Greek and Roman civilizations as well as the Mesopotamian and far eastern civilizations as far as India and China. Also, this system of spirituality spread to other parts of Africa and influenced the Yoruba and Dogon Religions among others. It had its greatest impact on the development of Christianity as the most important Christian rituals and myths incorporated the Ancient Egyptian teachings. Among these are the Eucharist, the resurrection and the virgin birth. Thus, Ancient Egyptian mystical religion and yoga are important sources for understanding and practicing all religions of modern times.

THE TREE STEPS OF RELIGION

In reality, the soul is in essence the heir of a higher identity which needs to be discovered and this is the real plan of nature and of religion. Religion has three levels of practice. These are *Myth, Ritual* and *Mystical Experience.* The mythical level encompasses the stories related to the deities of the religion and the names given to these are based on the specific culture and local folklore of the particular religious group in question. In order to practice religion fully it is necessary to have a connection to the religious symbols and icons and it is also necessary to understand the meaning of those symbols and icons. When this level is achieved then it is necessary to practice the rituals of the religion and to keep the traditions of the religion. This practice will allow a person to discover the deeper meaning of the philosophy contained in the myths. When the myths are understood and practiced a person can be lead to discover the deeper essence of the myth which transcends the outer or exoteric themes and plots of the story. In essence a person becomes the myth and in so doing he or she identifies with and discover the victory of the deity of the myth. Therefore, the first level relates to learning about the teachings. The second level relates to practicing them and the third level of religion relates to experiencing the teachings. Thus, in order to progress on the ladder of religion you need to regularly study the teachings and then attend the rituals of your community in relation to your religion. If this is not possible you should institute rituals in your home life which acknowledge and affirm the themes of the myth. See the audio and book presentations *How to Understand and Practice the Rituals of The Book of Coming Forth By Day* (audio cassette) and *The Ausarian Resurrection: The Ancient Egyptian Bible* (book) section entitled: "Incorporating the Osirian Rituals Into Your Life.

"The secrets of the universe cannot be discovered through study and research alone but the honest search for truth and the development of a incorruptible mind qualifies the seeker for higher instruction."

Ancient Egyptian Proverb

If a myth is only understood in its exoteric form, that is, without the true understanding of its purpose and meaning or even if it is understood intellectually but without practicing its teachings it is impossible to discover and experience the mystical realizations which it is leading to. Thus, a person becomes stuck in religious dogmatism and or intellectualism and this is the source of religious strife and animosity as well as the lack of understanding between peoples. In reality all true religions have these three levels but if a person is not able to discover these their spiritual growth is stunted as it were. (See *The Ausarian Resurrection: The Ancient Egyptian Bible*).

It is also important to understand that all true religions and yoga disciplines are aiming for the same goal even though they appear to be saying contradicting things in their outer form. Thus, you should develop a feeling of universality and freedom in the practice of religion. This will enable you to see the beauty of other traditions even while you concentrate on your own. This form of movement will also engender a spirit of goodwill an peace among different religious groups and this will allow all to develop inner peace and security in the company of others. Think of it as a pyramid. At the bottom there are four sides. These symbolize opposites. At the top there is a single point. This symbolizes universality and oneness. This is why in ancient times the great pyramids of Ancient Egypt had a capstone with the emblem of the Eye of Horus which represents transcendental spiritual vision which arises in a human being when the opposites (duality) are transcended. So too it is your duty to yourself and your offspring to move positively in the struggle of life and to triumph over ignorance and the negative qualities of the mind which lead to a dualistic view of life and spiritual dullness. Horus finally overcame Set in the Ausarian Resurrection myth by becoming *Ur-Uatchit* or all-encompassing and supremely full. This implies that he discovered his oneness with all that exists and all that exists is in God. Therefore he became one with God just as the Christian Bible text where Jesus says "I and the father are one" or the Hindu texts say "I am Brahman" or the Buddhists say "I am Buddha", etc. This means that you must grow in universality to see beyond the apparent differences which separate people from each other and to see the underlying thread which binds all. This movement will ultimately lead to your discovery of inner peace and inner fulfillment as well as your own spiritual enlightenment and that of your family.

As a parent it is incumbent upon you to study and practice the teachings of the religion you choose and to progress up the ladder of spirituality (three steps of religion) so that you may then lead your child to greater spiritual development as well. It would also be beneficial for you to become associated with an authentic spiritual preceptor and a spiritual community wherein you can freely study, practice the teachings and support each others efforts on a regular basis. Also, it would be beneficial for you to engage in an occupation which is meaningful, expresses your inner gifts and which serves humanity. This will allow you to expand your horizons and it will help you to eradicate the gross negativity within yourself (anger, hatred, greed and egoism). See *The Wisdom of Maati: Spiritual Enlightenment through the Path of Virtue.*

> "If your child accepts your words then no plan of theirs will go wrong. So teach your son to be a hearer, one who will be valued by the officials, one who will guide their speech by what they have been told, one who is regarded as a hearer. The children will reach old age if they listen to the wise words of their parents."
> Ancient Egyptian Proverb

Always treat your child with respect and answer all of his or her questions. If you don't know the answers find out through your own research and by interviewing advanced spiritual personalities. If they cannot answer your question to your satisfaction keep on searching. Also don't have your child do something you do not do yourself or believe in yourself. You should always feel that you are your child's spiritual preceptor and therefore, just as you accept and learn the teachings from a Sehu Neteru (Spiritual Preceptor) you should know that you are responsible for assimilating and then passing on the teaching not only to your child but to everyone you may come into contact with if they seek out your wisdom. The spreading of wisdom is not necessarily done in a preaching way but through your positive thoughts, words and deeds. Your very presence should inspire calm, confidence and joyousness. Then, when you are asked how you became so calm, contented and peaceful, you will be ready to respond to anyone who requests your wisdom.

The version of the Ausarian Resurrection that has been prepared for the children's book *The Story of Asar, Aset and Heru* contains many strong social issues and spiritual principles that should be discussed with your child. These include greed, violence and the pain and suffering of life. However, it also contains the essential wisdom of the ancients and the sublime vision of victory in the struggle of life and the blessings of spiritual enlightenment, inner peace, abiding joy and the possibility of discovering one's own innate divinity and immortality.

Heru the child.

PARENTING OR SPIRITUAL PARTNERSHIP

"Those who hath learned to know themselves, hath reached that Good which does transcend abundance; but they who through a love that leads astray, expend their love upon their body; they stay in Darkness wandering, and suffering through their senses things of Death."

Ancient Egyptian Proverb

Many times parents fall into the trap of attachment (*they who through a love that leads astray*) and egoistic desires in relation to their children. Your child does not, never will and never has belonged to you. So why treat them as possessions? Why bring them into the world only so that you can have someone to love or so that you can feel that you are having progeny and a legacy, or so that you can be proud of your virility or fertility or so that you can boast of their achievements which you were unable to accomplish, etc. These are all egoistic notions based on your own egoistic desires. At a higher level of spiritual experience you can discover that you are related to all children of the universe. This is what a Sage, a person who has matured in spirituality, experiences and this is why they do not feel the need to procreate in an ordinary manner. Rather, they discover that they can create wondrous works of spiritual literature and that they can affect the hearts of thousands of people with their mere presence when they have reached a certain state of spiritual purification.

Many people in modern society have developed the idea that it is good to depend on others as sources of happiness. They think it proper to live vicariously through their children. They see their own lives as unfulfilling and sometimes even as failures so they strive to push their children to succeed according to societies standards of success (money, fame, status, progeny, etc.) without understanding that these values are what led them (the parents) to the state in which they presently find themselves. But does this make any sense? Is it a good idea to place ones hopes on others who are subject to the whims of their own mentality as well as the unpredictability of life? You need to develop higher ideals for yourself which will lead you to discover your own purpose and your own fulfillment. When this occurs you will become a real source of wealth for the world and for your family. As a parent on the spiritual path you need to discover the joy of not depending on your child as a source of pleasure, pride or sentimental attachment. As you develop this quality of detachment from egoism and attachment to the spiritual essence of the heart you will be able to pass it on to your child. In so doing you will both develop a deeper form of love which goes beyond the superficial attachments which most people consider as the norm.

If you choose married life and the path of parenthood and want to also practice mystical spirituality this is possible if you see your life as a parent and your life as a wife or husband as a means to gathering the experiences which will help you to grow spiritually. This means that you will seek these relationships with people who will have the same goal and you will serve your family as you would serve humanity, selflessly and righteously without egoistic attachment and sentimentality based on ignorance and personal desires for sex or to be looked up to and admired as a producer of children as a breeding mare or bull.

Many times people misunderstand love with attachment and the prospect of fulfilling their own personal desires through their relationships. In so doing they lose the opportunity to build a strong and lasting relationship because egoistic desires can never be satisfied with an object or condition in the world of time and space. The human mind is in reality desiring something much higher than anything it can get from the world. This is why when relationships which are based on superficiality lose their novelty, passion or excitement people who fell in love with each other based on the egoistic ideals are eager to separate and move on in the search for more excitement. However, since they have not repaired the errors of their way of egoism they will only produce the same conditions with the next partner they encounter.* Since no partner can keep them excited all the time they will never discover true fulfillment or peace in their life and they will die as disappointed personalities. *(See *Egyptian Tantra Yoga: The Art of Sex Sublimation and Universal Consciousness*).

"Through firm instruction one can master one's emotions"

Ancient Egyptian Proverb

As a spiritual aspirant you must be perfectly clear on one point. You will never discover the higher levels of spiritual enlightenment if you hold on to egoistic attachments and desires be they related to objects or conditions of the world or to family members including your child. This also relates to the practice of spirituality. If you hold onto elementary teachings you will not be able to progress to more advanced teachings. Therefore, your vision must be higher than that of an ordinary parent. You must keep the prospective of growing to discover and see yourself and your child as spiritual beings and not as relations. In a higher sense you are both God's children so to speak and from an even higher perspective you are not related as parent and child but as the self same nature, the Divine. This also applies to your spouse and to every other human being on earth. The deepest reality is that you are related beyond any undoing. No distance, worldly condition or even death can untie the bonds between souls and between souls and God. Therefore, a new vision must emerge in the heart based on spiritual truth rather than egoistic sentiment.

In fact you must learn to be prepared to let them go at any time without feeling resentment or grief. In human life death can come at any time due to disease or accidents or other causes. Therefore, is it wise to hold something dear which can be taken away at a moments notice? Rather, you should learn to love your child's eternal and immortal essence, that which is imperishable and cannot be destroyed, the Divine essence within them. Also, you should learn to trust God who is working through nature, to lead them to the situations and circumstances they need to grow spiritually without resentment over something than may appear as bad or as good. People place these values on things but God sees them as good to the extent that they lead a human being towards spiritual evolution. To this end evil as well as good are only the means used to lead the soul towards self-discovery. In this manner you can also learn to forgive your child when they commit errors due to ignorance and egoism since you realize that it is ignorance operating and not the Divine Self within. Learn to accept the movements of nature as God's plan even while you strive to work towards bettering your life in all regards, spiritual and financial. Learn to develop detachment towards the feelings of selfishness and greed and don't seek to acquire more than is necessary for your needs. You will find that you will discover inner peace and contentment which will allow you to enter into greater and greater awareness of the spiritual reality which is all around you. As you become more and more spiritually aware your child will be exposed to your radiation of wisdom and courage. This inner spiritual strength will be a formidable force against the negativity of the outside world. You should encourage your child to cherish life as a precious gift from God but not in a sentimental way based on attachment and egoistic desires.

The mastery over one's emotions and desires is the cornerstone of spiritual realization. This exalted attainment is certainly possible. Very few people in history have discovered the joy of reaching a desireless state wherein there is no tension or anxiety over what one wants, what one strives to hold onto or cannot get. Great Sages throughout history have discovered this and they left their legacy in the form of the mystical religions and yoga philosophies from around the world for all peoples. Therefore, realize that you, as well as your child, have the potential to become great sages since the great figures of history were no different from you or your child. The difference is that they undertook the study and practice of the mystical teachings. So begin today to follow the royal road to spiritual enlightenment.

IMPARTING THE MYTH TO YOUR CHILD

"Every parent teaches as they act... They will set
an example and not give offence."
                    -Ancient Egyptian Proverb

If your child is an infant the matter of introducing them to the
teachings is simple. You simply need to live the teachings by
observing the rituals presented in the myth* and to uphold the
precepts of righteousness and truth in your own life. Also,
spiritual icons or symbols in your home environment will be
beneficial towards promoting the remembrance of spiritual
principles. As you progress in your own studies and as your child
observes you "living what you believe in" and benefiting from
your lifestyle he or she will naturally pick up on this as he or she
grows up.

If you have an older child and you wish to introduce yourself
and your child to the teachings you needn't burden them by trying
to force them to adhere to some new system overnight. You
should endeavor to be what you want them to become. This is the
first and most important factor in imparting the teachings. Be
righteous, compassionate, forgiving and loving. Your child will
respond to these more than force or scolding. Children see
through lies and deceit and they learn how to lie and be deceitful
or righteous and upstanding from the people whom they accept as
being the role models in their life. Therefore, seek out every
opportunity to be in the company of those who are practicing,
professing and promoting the teachings. Also, discover for
yourself and show your child how the mystical teachings you are
discovering can also be found in your previous religion. This way
of approaching spirituality will open the doors to all that is good
in any system of spirituality. This is the practice of universal
religion.

"To have peace there must be strife; both are part
of the structure of the world and requirements for
the instruction of the children of GOD."
                    -Ancient Egyptian Proverb

Never forget that your child, like yourself, is an eternal soul on a journey to self-discovery. They have purposely come to this world with all its faults and they will sometimes go astray as you did once. Also never forget that the Divine hand is watching over them and that sometimes a soul needs to make mistakes, experience suffering and disappointment in order to grow and develop. Your role is to do your best to be a role model to the extent of your capacity and then to allow Neteru (The Supreme Being or *Pa Neter* expressing as the cosmic forces of nature) to lead them along the path which they need to experience. Many times parents feel regrets and consider themselves as failures if their children go astray even when they made major efforts to control or give guidance to their child. Also, sometimes parents allow their guilt feelings to be manipulated by their child who makes them feel bad in order to get something out of them and to support their unrighteousness. This is a form of parental ignorance because you as a parent are not all knowing, all-seeing, all-powerful, etc. so why treat yourself that way. This is essentially an expression of lack of faith and egoism because you are taking upon yourself the burden which really belongs to God. If you truly believe in God you must accept life as it comes, knowing that there is a higher wisdom operating. *See *The Ausarian Resurrection, The Ancient Egyptian Bible* and *Mysticism of Ushet Rekhat: Worship of The Divine Mother* and *Introduction to the Book of Coming Forth By Day* for more on practicing the teachings and rituals of Shetaut Asar (the Ausarian Resurrection Religion).

The children's book *The Story of Asar, Aset and Heru* is designed for use as a coloring book. So you may encourage your child to personalize it in any way they choose.

HEALTH AND NUTRITION

There are many dimensions to health and nutrition. Most importantly health is first a mental quality and then a physical one. If you practice the teachings outlined above you are in the process of taking care of the mental aspect. Next you will need to take care of the physical. The ancient teachings of the Temple of Aset (Isis) and the mystical literature of yoga have included guidelines as to diet and nutrition.* Generally, you should promote a vegetarian diet and a healthy physical activity schedule including yoga exercises. *See Initiation Into Egyptian Yoga.

The Ausarian Resurrection is the basis of the *Thef Neteru* or the Egyptian Yoga Exercise workout program.* For young children it is not necessary to have them practice a daily regimen of physical exercises but it will be sufficient if they are encouraged to imitate the postures of the Thef Neteru (Gods and goddesses) of the Ausarian myth. This is a uniquely positive way to teach them the myth. In a storytelling format they can participate by assuming the postures of the gods and goddesses as they hear of their activities. In fact, this is the practice of the first and second steps of religion (myth and ritual) being experienced at the same time. Older children may feel a calling to intensify their efforts in this direction. This should be encouraged but never forced on a child. Once again, if they see you doing it they will also want to do it as well. *See the book *Egyptian Yoga Exercise Workout Book.*

CHANTING AND MEDITATION

Chanting is a very easy way to promote closeness and at the same time positive awareness with your child. Even if your child does not understand the meaning of the chants they will engender a positive feeling towards life and spiritual practice. As you practice the chants you will develop greater insight, inner peace and will power in your own life. This will also affect your child as he or she develops greater spiritual strength (establishment in the teachings), and will power to resist the temptations of life. Chanting the Divine Name is an easy way to change the vibrations of the mind from positive to negative and to promote remembrance of God. Also it is a good way to promote closeness between your child and God. The chants may take the form of those traditionally prescribed or you may create songs and other special names which relate your child to the form of god (Aset, Heru, Asar, Ra, etc.) with which they feel most resonance with.*

Meditation is a more advanced practice which you should certainly practice according to your increasing level of spiritual development. A child needn't be burdened with sitting quietly for long periods of time. However short periods will be beneficial in giving them an understanding that life does not have to be a constant movement from the time they wake up to the time they go to bed. This will make it easier for them to practice formal meditation later on in their life when they are ready.*
*See *Meditation: The Ancient Egyptian Path to Enlightenment.*

The Maati goddesses: forms of Aset and Nebthet symbolizing double truth, righteousness, etc.

TOPICS FOR DISCUSSION WITH YOUR CHILD

This final section will include some themes you may wish to introduce to your child through the medium of the Ausarian myth. It is designed for use with the children's book: *The Story of Asar, Aset and Heru.*

THE CREATION

The creation of the world and the universe is a most important teaching to be understood by everyone. The primeval ocean theme was used by many spiritual philosophies. Most notably by the Hindus and the Christians. However, it appears first and most prominent in Ancient Egyptian mythology and there it carries a special connotation. The ocean symbolizes the potential for creation and it represents a metaphor relating to the body of God itself. The Universe is not separate from God. Rather, God has transformed him/her self into Creation so that people may have place to grow spiritually. Therefore, explain to your child that the universe is like the waves of an ocean and that everything is Divine. The God Nu is God manifesting as the ocean of potential, unmanifest matter and from this unmanifest, the manifest world of time and space has arisen just as a dream emerges from the mind when you sleep. For more on this theme see the books *The Ausarian Resurrection, God In The Universe, God In The Heart* and *The Hidden Properties of Matter.*

THE EMERGENCE OF RA

God is in reality the soul of the ocean as well as the ocean itself. However, in its unmanifest state the ocean is formless and vast. but in order to lead a person to understand God the ancient Sages enjoined the practice of using symbolic forms to express ideas. Thus, they created the symbol of wavy lines symbolizing the primeval ocean and the form of Ra and placed him on a boat sailing on the ocean along with nine gods and goddesses. These gods and goddesses represent important principles or characteristics about creation. These characteristics include the constituent elements of which nature is composed and also the nature of the human mind. This section of the story immediately introduces the theme of a universal being from which all things emanate and are controlled. This spiritual philosophy from Ancient Egypt is sometimes referred to as monotheistic or polytheistic but these terms are incorrect because monotheism relates to a God who "creates" Creation and polytheism refers to a system of many gods who exist independently. The body of God itself is Creation. Therefore, this refers to a pantheistic and panentheistic understanding of Divinity which is very advanced indeed.

Pantheism means: 1- Absolute Pantheism: Everything there is, is God. 2- Modified Pantheism: God is the reality or principle behind nature.

Panentheism means: that God is immanent in all things but also transcendent, so that every part of the universe has its existence in God; but God is more than the sum total of the parts.

Thus, the universe is not a haphazard phenomenon but it is based on a well thought out and managed concept which is sustained by one Supreme Being who is not in some distant corner of the universe but as close as the next touch or even the next thought. Therefore, discuss these principles as they are introduced in the book in accordance with your level of understanding and to the extent than your child can grasp them. Discus the symbolic wisdom behind Neter (god or goddess) with your child.

RA, THE SUPREME BEING AND CREATOR

As discussed earlier, the depiction of the Supreme Being in mystical religion is not meant as an absolute rendering. God is transcendental of all forms. However, forms are used to lead the mind until such time as it is strong enough to think of God without any form while encompassing all forms. It is like using crutches until the leg is healed and you can walk on your own again. Another important idea here is that God encompasses both male and female. God is the singularity from which the duality (complementary opposites) in the form of male and female gods and goddesses as well as male and female human beings has emerged. The soul is without sex just as Divinity is sexless. However, souls have attached themselves to a form in time and space and all forms in time and space must exist in duality. However, the soul is never transformed into duality but it believes itself to be male or female, rich or poor, desirable or undesirable in accordance with the level of ignorance and delusion in the mind. Thus, both sexes are to be seen for what they are, modes of divine expression. Since all expressions in time and space (duality) are not perfect, men and women have faults but they can also manifest goodness and perfection to the extent that they are established in the Higher Self rather than in egoism. So you should promote openness, fairness and acceptance of gender and in this manner begin to see people not as individual sex beings but as spiritual beings to be loved equally. See the book *God in the Universe, God in the Heart.*

MAAT

Many volumes could be written about the principle of Maat. Maat is a cosmic force as well as a spiritual philosophy of life which is based on order, righteousness, justice and correctness. Ancient Egyptian civilization was based on the concept of Maat and the Ancient Egyptian Creation story shows that Maat was the very first principle to be established. Maat is known as the daughter of Ra. She represents the very energy which holds the various elements of matter in their place, the physical laws and the laws of chemistry which allow scientist to plan the way in which to use materials and to predict how chemicals will interact. How would life exist if water flows up into the sky instead of down to the ocean or if the earth is gaseous and cannot hold plants, etc.?

Any person who lives according to the principles of Maat will discover peace, prosperity and truth in their life and they will promote harmony in society as well as spiritual enlightenment for all people. If there is no order and righteousness there cannot be any life because chaos and disorder are against progress and evolution. A child must understand that for every action they perform there will be a result. Therefore, "what you do comes back to you" in other words. Thus, Maat also implies the teaching of karma. They need to have a basis for acting righteously and for recognizing what is righteous versus what is not. They should know that goddess Maat is always watching over them wherever they might be and that she will always let them suffer the consequences of their actions, be they positive or negative. Further, goddess Maat is always there to assist them in acting rightly. So when there is a question about what is right or wrong action they can think of the goddess and how Heru triumphed by acting rightly and they will know the correct path to follow. See the book *The Wisdom of Maati: Enlightenment Through the Path of Virtue.*

SHU AND TEFNUT

Shu and Tefnut are the next principles established by God in order to bring forth Creation. Shu not only represents air and atmosphere but space itself. If there is no space nothing can exist because there is no place for it to exist. When you dream you are actually creating space in your mind, a place in which to carry out your dream. In the same way, God has created the space of this universe in order to allow the objects (planets, stars, etc.) of his/her dream to exist.

Tefnut is commonly referred to as moisture but she is much more than that. Her iconography which includes the lioness, the serpent on the crown of the head, the papyrus scepter and the ankh holds important mystical symbolism. These icons symbolize the power of nature (lioness), life (ankh), the papyrus scepter symbolizes among other things the power of knowledge. The serpent symbolizes the power of the Life Force energy which courses through nature and which sustains all life. When it is placed on the crown of the head it signifies that the power has reached full expression. It is related to the discipline known as

Serpent Power Yoga or the cultivation of the internal Life Force energy. When this discipline is taken to completion a human being can develop his or her individual Life Force and then join it with the Universal Life Force (God) and thereby attain spiritual enlightenment. This is a process which occurs naturally in all human beings as they experience life and reincarnation. However, when yoga is practiced the process of spiritual evolution is enhanced and accelerated. See the book *The Serpent Power: The Development of the Internal Life Force.*

GEB and NUT

Have you wondered why everything in the universe expresses as opposites? Think about it, people animals, insects, plants express as male and female. There is a universal principle in nature and this principle has been recognized by mystical philosophy and expressed in the forms of the neters or gods and goddesses of Ancient Egypt as well as those of Hindu mythology. Geb and Nut symbolize the second phase of creation and Shu and Tefnut represent the first. Shu and Tefnut represent the subtle forces behind Creation and Geb and Nut represent the phase of nature which expresses as the gross elements of nature, namely, the physical earth and the heavens with the planets and stars, etc.

Thus, the creation part of the myth relates us to nature in a very special way. The deeper meaning is that Creation itself is related to God in a direct way, as son and daughter and not as a subject - object relationship such as a person who might create a pot or a work of sculpture, etc. Thus, discuss this marvelous fact with your child and discover the wondrous nature of creation together.

THE CHILDREN OF GEB AND NUT

Asar, Aset, Set and Nebthet relate to the psychology of the human mind. Asar relates to the soul. Aset relates to wisdom, love, devotion and the regenerative capacity for healing in the body. Set relates to egoism, violence and uncontrolled brute force and Nebthet relates to the physical aspect of a human being, the body and mortality. The profound teachings related to these themes would require volumes in order to do them justice. Therefore it is strongly suggested that you see the books: *The Ausarian Resurrection: The Ancient Egyptian Bible* and *The Mystical Teachings of The Ausarian Resurrection: Initiation Into The Third Level of Shetaut Asar.*

Another important feature of the story is the importance of the balance between the sexes. In modern times the denigration of the female gender has caused untold misery and the disintegration of the family. Anyone who intends to raise a child needs to provide positive male and female role models who have a mutual feeling of acceptance and self-worth. This means that mature and spiritually aware men and women must honor each other as equal partners in life as well as in parenting. They must see each other as two souls who have come together to help each other and their family to grow spiritually. Further, they need to see each others roles as complementary and not adversarial or competitive. In this manner they will develop a strong appreciation for each other, their family and their relationship to the spirit (God).

If men and women do not uphold these ideals their relationship degrades into a feeling that marriage is a forum where personal pleasures are to be satisfied through sex or service from the partner. Since no one can fully satisfy any other person, partners who pursue this philosophy of pleasure seeking are soon disappointed in each other and they become mentally and or physically unfaithful and they begin to blame each other and hurt each other in various ways. Sometimes they hurt each other through their children and this hurt leaves negative impressions on the child and when the child grows up they too begin the cycle of negativity because they too do not think about the folly of selfishness and the indiscriminate pursuit to fulfill egoistic desires.

In reality, spiritual life is a life of sacrifice. But this does not mean that it is without joy. When the egoism of the mind, ignorance and negativity are sacrificed in favor of inner peace, sharing, forgiveness, universal love and wisdom the experience is of a greater joy than any worldly development can provide. This experience does not diminish relationships. It brings greater depth and happiness to them. For more on relationships and the spiritual life see the book *Egyptian Tantra Yoga: The art of Sex Sublimation and Universal Consciousness.*

RA CREATES HUMAN BEINGS

This is a very important theme of the creation. Human beings sometimes feel a disconnection from nature and from God. This condition is exacerbated by the philosophies like the evolutionary theory and humanism and others which hold that human beings are just physical entities who come from apes, or the earth, etc.

Think of what the texts is saying. It actually states that human beings are direct descendents of the Supreme Being, not unlike the neters. Therefore, every human being is a divine expression of God and it is painful to God to see human beings going on their way, not remembering who they are and where they came from. Thus, discuss these themes daily with your child.

God is most pleased and gratified when he/she is remembered as the very source and sustenance of life. This practice of remembrance leads to a deep sense of joy and this level of spiritual experience is referred to as "bliss." An easy way to remember God is to read spiritual literature daily, to chant the Divine Name (Om Asar-Aset-Heru), to practice meditation on the Self (God) daily and all of the other rituals of mystical religion and the disciplines of yoga. See the book *Meditation: The Ancient Egyptian Path to Enlightenment* and *Initiation Into Egyptian Yoga.*

TEHUTI AND SESHETA

It is important to understand the principles that these two neters represent. Think about your own mind. When you have a thought where does it come from? It comes from the innermost reaches of your unconscious mind or you might also consider this as the soul. But how is this thought formed? It is formed when a deep impression of your unconscious emerged into your subconscious and conscious mind just like a bubble rises from the deeper part of the ocean up to the surface.

In the same way your thoughts have a source, the unconscious, and your subconscious and conscious minds translate those impressions into thought concepts, feelings and desires. Lets say that the soul has a need to expand and to discover happiness. This impression translates into the various thoughts about acquiring objects or seeking favorable circumstances in life.

So Ra-Asar is the source of all knowledge and Tehuti and Sesheta are the cosmic mind (mind of God) which translate the wisdom and divine pronouncements into divine law. These pronouncements or ordinations from the divine relate to the forces which keep nature orderly, the Life Force which sustains all life, the spiritual assistance which people need from time to time as well as the various injunctions of wisdom and righteousness known as the philosophy of Maat in Ancient Egypt and otherwise known as the Ten Commandments and the Beatitudes of Christianity and the Dharma of the Hindus and Buddhists, etc.

Therefore, practice the art of reasoning with your child and you will assist in the development of theirs and your reasoning capacity which is necessary for studying and understanding the Divine as well as for success in any other endeavor of life. See the book *The Hymns of Amun.*

ASAR AND ASET TRAVEL THE WORLD

This is a very important theme of the Ausarian Resurrection myth. The actual ancient scriptures tell of the travels of Asar (Osiris) throughout Asia (Europe, India and China) and Ausarian artifacts have been found in other parts of Africa as well. Also, the Dogon peoples of West Africa acknowledge their lineage to the Ancient Egyptians. Therefore, there is a historical basis to show that in ancient times the Egyptian culture touched the farthest reaches of the ancient world. This explains why the religions of different countries in ancient times carry so many features which were practiced by the Ancient Egyptians. It also explain why the present day world religions still carry on the same traditions which were first practiced in Ancient Egyptian Religion. Thus, never cease to reinforce this factor when discussing the similarities to other religions and when teaching history to your child. This theme lends authenticity and primacy to Ancient Egyptian religion which should not be used for denigrating other religions but as a means to legitimizing its study along side other religious traditions in your own mind and in the minds of others. This theme will allow people to see that there is a common thread among religions and that this knowledge leads to greater understanding and harmony among religions and a greater understanding of the depth of all religions.

THE MURDER OF ASAR

There are many important themes to be found here. Children should learn about death as soon as possible. In this manner they may develop a true appreciation for life. Also, they should not learn of it first from people who are twisted and devoid of spiritual insight or those who are caught up in materialism and the mentality of violence or from the news or entertainment media. In reality death is not a finality but a facet of the journey of the soul which must be understood by everyone on the spiritual path.

First, the matter of Asar's killing by his own brother is compelling since it is someone so close to him. The similarity to the Biblical story of Cain and Able is evident. The deeper symbolism relates to the fact that egoism (Set) kills the soul (Asar) as it were. Egoism is the feeling of individuality and selfishness which arises when one forgets where one comes from and who is sustaining the world. Egoism is the idea of self importance and aggrandizement and Set is the symbol of the ego. Asar is killed but this is only a physical death. The soul cannot be killed. It only travels on its journey to another world, another family and another incarnation into another body until it finally remembers its true identity. This is the teaching of reincarnation and karma which are very important teachings of Ancient Egyptian Religion.

This is also an excellent place to introduce the theme of real happiness. Everyone, all creatures in the world are searching for happiness and everyone wants to avoid pain but how is this possible? The mass mentality says that happiness is to be found in wealth and fame (egoism) so since the modern world has so many wealthy and famous people we should be able to find allot of happiness should we not? There are many wealthy and famous people in the world and they are still plagued by the tensions, stresses and disappointments of life. Therefore, happiness is not in wealth and fame, nor is it in relationships or in the fulfillment of desires. No matter how much you love someone there will always be some pain associated with a relationship if it is engaged in at an egoistic level. The person will eventually do something that will upset you and ultimately they will die and this will cause great pain.

Many people feel that if all their desires could be fulfilled they would be happy but this is not realistic since it is not possible to fulfill all of a person's desires. How can the infinite and eternal soul be satisfied with anything that is not infinite and eternal? Further, the fulfillment of one desire gives rise to another desire and there will always be some tension associated with the pursuit of desire fulfillment. When a person seems to discover a little happiness when they acquire something they get greedy and want more or become jealous of those who have more. So where is true and abiding happiness?

You have a wonderful opportunity to set your child on the right road to happiness. Happiness is already present in the innermost reaches of a person's being. It can be discovered when a person finds the essence of who they are and it begins to manifest as soon as a person begins to discover the insanity of a life based on egoism and desires. The reason there seems to be such force in the direction of desire fulfillment in the world is that the real urge within a person is not understood by by most people. The real urge is to discover themselves but through ignorance of the higher reality and lack of awareness of a better way a person begins to search for happiness in worldly objects and relationships which are limited and perishable. Objects and relationships are means to an end and not ends in themselves. Through them a person can learn to value what is real, abiding and eternal, the essence within them and which sustains them (God). This essence can be easily discovered when there is peace of mind (Hetep) and peace of mind comes when there is right understanding and when life is based on righteousness (Maat) instead of egoism and mental agitations due to the pursuit of sensual pleasures from objects and egoistic relationships. Thus you should impart this great wisdom to your child through your actions and your discussions with them.

Desires, longings and cravings are the road to worldliness, and stress. They allow the negative aspects of the mind to emerge and intensify. In short, the root of desires is egoism and the root of egoism is ignorance of the true Self. The Soul or innermost Self, is the source of all happiness and therefore it is the place to seek fulfillment of desires and until a person becomes introspective and desireless he or she will not discover true peace and happiness. Desires are in reality a degradation or slavery for the soul and when people are given gifts and when they are expected to feel "happy" it is a reinforcement of the illusion that happiness is in an object that can be acquired. Attachment to objects is also a degrading development because they drain the mental energy so that a person's thoughts, aspirations and desires are directed towards and wasted on the pursuit something that is a waste of time and energy. This leads to diminished mental capacity for reasoning and reduced will to resist worldly temptations.

Worldly desires arise when there is wrong understanding in the mind as to the true means to fulfill the need of the soul which is to know itself. Worldly desires and attachments can be reduced when a person begins to understand that physical objects and even the body, mind and senses are in reality expressions of God, the intellect begins to realize "why should I desire what I already have." As this ideal is understood intellectually it gradually leads to increasing levels of peace, tranquility and contentment even as a person continues to participate in the world. As this movement matures a desire arises to purify oneself mentally and physically in order to experience greater inner discovery. This means promoting positive thoughts and consuming pure foods and abstaining from negative associations, negative thoughts and poisonous substances such as cigarettes, meat and drugs.

It must be clearly understood that when we speak of "becoming desireless" from a spiritual point of view this does not mean becoming like an uncaring personality or a lifeless mannequin. Desirelessness implies not living life according to egoistic desires and expectations. It means living according to a higher wisdom which allows a person to be happy whether or not things work out to their advantage or not. It means realizing that internally and externally God pervades all and is therefore present everywhere. It means developing an awareness of the depth within oneself and the feeling of divine love which emanates from the heart. When a person depends on or holds expectations from things outside of him or her as a source of happiness they are headed for sure disappointment and they will never have inner peace because the tension of expectation never lets the mind rest. If a person begins to depend on that which is unchanging and pure their need for outside sources of pleasure will be reduced. When this occurs a person's desires gradually become purified. That is to say, their desires are not egoistic and their expectations are in line with the necessities of life and of nature. This means that such a person does not desire for wealth which they do not need but only for so much as they may need to take care of their practical realities. When desires and expectations are in line with righteousness their fulfillment occurs automatically. Further, such a person may expect a tangible result from their work in the form of a paycheck but they will not expect to be praised or worshipped and likewise their internal establishment in the innermost Self will protect them from curses and censure from others. All of this is possible because they are internally established in the highest truth and this is the only approval they require. This way of living leads to inner peace, contentment and spiritual insight because as the mind experiences deeper and deeper levels of peace a person is able to go deeper into the depths of the heart. This is true spiritual self-discovery.

This movement ultimately leads to the awareness of oneness with God and this feeling transcends all worldly experiences, all concepts of worldly happiness and all concepts of worldly desires. It is important to understand that spiritual life ultimately needs to transcend even spiritual concepts and outer forms of spiritual practice because the soul is beyond concepts and spiritual practice is only a concept based on the spiritual experiences of Sages and Saints. So from ignorance a person has been led to positive desires and aspirations and towards wisdom instead of imaginations and delusion. Ultimately they are led to the height of spiritual experience wherein there is an awareness of God everywhere and in all things and that God is the source of happiness, love and peace, the very essence of all that exists (Neberdjer).

Seldom do people reflect on the erroneous logic of modern culture and the mass mentality of materialism and egoism. Consequently people seldom understand or experience what it is like to not have egoistic desires in the mind and to discover real inner peace and inner fulfillment. If they are confronted with this ideal they even refuse to think about it because they are so caught up in the delusion of desires and ignorance. Even though your child may not be able to grasp some of these enlightening concepts he or she can certainly feel their subtle influence through you and your lifestyle. Eventually, what they learned as a children's story will grow in deeper and deeper levels of depth as they grow older and eventually they will have an easy time reading and studying more extensive texts of the actual scripture since they have had a strong basis from their early days.

It is important to understand that spiritual life is not about self-denial or some morbid idea of renouncing happiness and comfort. It is the process of discovering what is truly fulfilling, liberating and meaningful in life and giving up those things which lead to bondage and pain.

The two goddesses Aset and Nebthet are bewailing and mourning over the death of Asar. One meaning is that the gross (Nebthet) and subtle (Aset) parts of nature feel what happens in human existence. Nothing goes unnoticed and nothing is without value, purpose and meaning in nature. The deeper implications of this factor are revealed in the next sections.

THE NETERS SEARCH FOR ASAR

The two goddesses Aset and Nebthet set out to find the body of Asar with the help of Apuat and Sebek. Apuat is the deity who represents clear vision and mental determination which allows a person to see right from wrong and to accomplish the goal of discovering the Divine Self (Asar). Sebek is a crocodile god and he represents the vicious force of the animal kingdom when it is tamed and its force is channeled towards a positive goal in life. The most positive goal a person can have in life is to discover their true essence and the nature of Creation. This stage also refers to the fact that when a person grows spiritually the forces in nature which seemed inimical and which appeared to overpower a person (lower self and its desires) are the same forces which he or she can use to promote spiritual evolution. How much energy would you have to practice meditation if you could break the desire for going out to parties every night?

Therefore, discuss the idea that nature is here to assist us in our life. It is not an enemy or a hindrance to be put up with. First the nature within ourselves in the form of ego must be mastered. This implies controlling desires, impatience, emotions and physical exuberance. This process may take time but it can occur if you truly "desire" it. The same force which pulled you towards worldliness and vice can pull you towards virtue. Next the nature outside of us can also be mastered. Thus, the need for self-control should be impressed at an early age even as you allow your child to have experiences which will provide an opportunity for them to find out for themselves the wisdom of what you are saying. During the early years a child's environment should be strictly controlled but as the child grows older they need to have experiences in the world in which they can test what they have learned at home. This testing process is nature's way of allowing a person to discover their inner capacities and inner gifts to overcome their own negative qualities in order to lead themselves to greater spiritual enlightenment.

FINDING THE BODY OF ASAR

"The body belongs to the earth and the soul belongs to heaven"

Ancient Egyptian Proverb

When the body of a human being dies it becomes inert like a rock or a piece of metal. This is because the soul or the individual ray of consciousness, has left it and along with it the Life Force energy which sustains the body has also gone away. When death occurs the body decomposes and goes back to the earth. It is assimilated and recycled so that it may become the food for another animal in the form of plants and fruits.

Asar's body is special. His body is the life force itself which sustains Creation and it is Creation itself as well. Thus, it is depicted as a mummy out of which plants are growing and also as a pillar with four tiers which symbolize the psycho-spiritual energy centers of consciousness and the Serpent Power energy also known as Kundalini.

At this point you may discuss with your child that while the body dies it is not destroyed but only transformed into a new condition. The spirit or that which is the essence of a human being remains and it is this that Aset recognizes and discovers. She achieves this great find because of her wisdom, devotion and love for the Divine (Asar). She can recognize it wherever it may be because Aset (wisdom) knows where to find what is good and true.

Thus, the virtues of Aset, wisdom, devotion and love should be praised and celebrated in your household and these ideals should be promoted as desirable as opposed to attaining material success beyond the necessary means or pleasure seeking and frivolous entertainment. Once again, if your child sees that you are benefiting from the cultivation of these virtues, they will feel the same way as you do about them. Even if they may go astray as many children do in the difficult process of growing up eventually they will remember the experiences of their youth and in one way or another they will one day turn towards the teachings you have provided.

ASET PRAYS OVER ASAR

This stage of the story implies the importance of spiritual practice. If spiritual practice is limited to dry intellectualism without feeling or blind faith and empty rituals (ignorance of their meaning and purpose) the true inner discovery of spiritual life will not be possible.

The fruit of Aset's prayers and meditations is the birth of Heru. This symbolizes the birth of spiritual awareness and growing spiritual enlightenment in the life of a spiritual aspirant when he or she begins to discover the spiritual essence in their life. Therefore, you should maintain a regular schedule of spiritual practices daily and not just once a week. Spiritual practice (Sheti) should be daily if it is to be successful. See the book *Initiation Into Egyptian Yoga: The Secrets of Sheti*.

THE BIRTH OF HERU

The birth of a spiritual leader is an auspicious event. Many religions have described it in various ways. The birth relates to a specific mystical symbolism which relates to the manner in which a spiritual aspirant may propitiate the birth of spiritual development in their own life. First of all the mother is Aset, who represents wisdom, love and devotion. Notice beside her on the right is Tehuti, holding a sistrum. This instrument is related, among other things, to the four elements of creation and the four psycho-spiritual consciousness centers described earlier and their stirring or awakening. This implies physical fitness and a balanced development in personality along with spiritual practice, the development of reason and spiritual studies. On the other side is the god Amun who is holding the Ankh (life) and the Uas scepter, the symbol of flowing Life Force. He is imparting Heru with the life and power of the universe. Amun represents the potential of every spiritual aspirant when they tap into the very source of life which is hidden in the Higher Self.

ASET AND HERU RUN AWAY

This part of the ancient story is similar in most respects to the story of the flight of Mary and Jesus in the Christian Bible. In order for a spiritual birth to occur in your heart your spiritual life must be protected and sheltered from the storms of emotions and the negativity of the mind (anger, hatred, greed, lust, jealousy, etc.) and of the world. In time the spiritual consciousness develops to a degree wherein a person is ready to face the world. This is the objective of every human being. So there is no need to test one's spiritual attainments or to openly profess teachings in the beginning which will draw challenges and ridicule from those who are spiritually ignorant and immature. This would only cause useless mental agitation and distraction.

ASET AND ASAR EDUCATE HERU

Before Heru could grow up and face Set he needed to be groomed and well schooled. Both Aset and Asar taught him all he needed to know so that he would be able to challenge Set successfully. The ego cannot be confronted directly until there is a high degree of spiritual maturity and training. A person can easily fool themselves on the spiritual path. They could be thinking that they are being spiritual because they are talking to others about the teachings while harboring a desire and for being praised, worshipped and singled out as a "special" person. All the while there is egoism and when someone disagrees with them or does not praise them in a way they are used to they become angry and agitated. This is not true spiritual practice.

Therefore, you should always strive to teach yourself and your child the important spiritual principles of life while at the same time maintaining a sense of humility. Always remember that what you know is not coming from you but from the Higher Self and all credit should go to it instead of to the ego. This process includes being honest with your child about your own life, your mistakes and also the wisdom which you have gained from the teachings. Your children will not think less of you if you are a student of the teachings and still make mistakes. They will be more forgiving because they will have a deeper understanding of the reasons why people act the way they do and they will know how to help others in their time of need. In this manner you and your child can learn from each other as you help each other on the spiritual path. The wisdom teachings are best imparted and handed down when they are taught by someone who has experienced them first hand. Therefore, as you begin to discover the wisdom of the spiritual teachings you will become a most effective Spiritual Preceptor for your child and for everyone who comes into contact with you.

This is also a good place to talk about the benefits of a vegetarian diet. Scientific studies have shown that meat eating and the consumption of processed foods leads not only to disease but also to mental instability, aggressiveness and agitation. Is it any wonder that once a person becomes ill or as they grow older they are told to eat less meat and to add more fiber to their diet? Also, meat eating promotes violence on animals. How can a person say that they live by truth and nonviolence if they promote the killing of animals so that they can experience the pleasure of consuming them. Scientific evidence also shows that meat eating is not necessary for health. All of this wisdom was known to the Ancient Egyptians and this philosophy was taught in their temples and the spiritual initiates were all vegetarians.* Therefore, vegetarianism should be promoted from a very early age. See *Initiation Into Egyptian Yoga: The Secrets of Sheti.*

CONFRONTING SET

The most important point here is the fact of standing up for what is right. Many people feel that nonviolence means being quiet in the face of evil and unrighteousness or that a "spiritual person" should be always gentle and quiet. This is an immature view. Spiritual strength implies strong ethical understanding and strong willpower which allow a person to uphold the higher ideals at a time of temptation or trial. When confronting evil, violence should never be contemplated. One should confront evil when one is strong enough to stand up to it with the power of reason, forgiveness, love and goodwill. Egoism, evil and the negative aspects of the mind arise only when there is ignorance of the spiritual truth. Therefore, you should remain compassionate towards those who cannot control themselves. Violence can be used only as a last resort when evil threatens the existence of righteousness and truth but always with the idea of stopping, controlling and re-educating the evil so as to sublimate it into the good and not with the idea of destroying and eradicating it. Also, it should not be confronted with anger and hatred or with resentment. These negative aspects of the mind consume a person regardless of the cause. If this ideal is not followed and a person indulges in anger and hatred in order to fight evil, they themselves will also become evil because anger and hatred and their emotions, thoughts and feelings are the way to becoming selfish, callous, destructive and evil.

THE TEST OF LIFE

Life tests a spiritual aspirants attainment in various ways. There are always going to be situations where a person's patience and fortitude will be tested. Sometimes a person will discover that they failed to keep calm or that they lost control and said something they should not have. This happens even to those who follow the spiritual teachings in the beginning. This is to be expected. A child cannot control their mind and body in the beginning with the myriads of desires and burgeoning thoughts as they discover the world. Added to this what of the karmic impressions from past lifetimes? So what can be said of an older person who has lived many years following the path of negativity and ignorance, and has never tried to control the emotions and the negative aspects of the mind?

You should take heart in the fact that all spiritual teachers, even the greatest ones such as Asar, Jesus, Buddha, Krishna, etc. have suffered through the same problems of life and look at what they accomplished. This can be the result in your life as well if you strive to live as they did. Strive to direct your life towards the Divine and the power of the Divine will rush to your side to help you with all your difficult trials.

This section points to the need for spending quiet time to reflect upon things. If the mind is constantly bombarded with thoughts and emotions the reasoning and will capacities will be impaired. Therefore, it is wise to regularly spend time quietly reflecting upon the teachings, reflecting upon the trials of life and one's actions and reflecting upon the higher ideals of life. So turn off the television and disconnect the telephone and have your child take a nap or spend some quiet time with you for a certain period during the day.

GOD COMES TO HELP HERU

The most important theme here is that when a person is in need, God in the form of nature, people and sometimes mysterious forces, comes to assist a person to face adversity. Adversity is a situation in which people grow spiritually if they face it with faith and honesty. Thus, Heru was assisted by Hathor and Tehuti, who restored Heru's vision by bringing him spiritual strength (Hathor) and reason for intuitional vision (Tehuti) so that he (Heru) might see that Set is not more powerful than wisdom and righteousness so all he (Heru) has to do is to stand firm in righteousness (Maat) without yield to emotionality and despair in order to prevail.

HERU AND SET GO TO COURT

There are several important themes here. First, it is remarkable that the court did not know what to do about the conflict. This points to the fact that God supports good as well as evil. All people, creatures and other life forms on earth come from the same source, God. Therefore, if one person is acting negatively towards another it must be because they are ignorant as to this spiritual wisdom. Their egoism has taken over and their ability to reason and control themselves has been impaired. So the need here is to understand that conflict and adversity occur in the lives of those who are virtuous as well as those who are inimical for the purpose of leading them both to greater heights of spiritual awareness through their interactions.

The court of gods and goddesses was confused and intimidated by Set. This points to the fact that when egoism gets out of hand with the yelling, screaming and carrying on: "I want," "I desire," "This is mine," etc., the noise and agitation impairs the mind's thinking process and it cannot reason properly. It is caught up in the delusion and illusions based on ignorance.

So the court sought higher counsel and the answer was that they should remember to do Maat (what is right). So too a spiritual aspirant should remember to seek higher counsel when the answers to a problem are not forthcoming or when the mind is hard to control. This can be accomplished through prayer, chanting, meditation, exercise, obtaining counseling from and listening to spiritual discourses from authentic spiritual preceptors and various other spiritual disciplines. Also, in the absence of a specific course of action to solve a problem righteousness is always the best general course of action.

Always encourage your child to seek you out for counseling and always remain somewhat detached from your ego so that you may be able to listen without being judgmental. Everyone wants to be understood and listened to with openness and honesty. If you provide this forum for your child your relationship will grow and become stronger with time. You will be able to face adversities together without the need to seek out ignorant friends, drugs, food, or other immature methods of coping with situations of life.

HERU IS CROWNED

If all of the teachings outlined here are practiced they will lead a spiritual aspirant to the highest goals of spiritual realization. This implies being crowned with the knowledge and wisdom of self-discovery and to be given the riches of the kingdom of inner peace, contentment and infinite joy. This is what Heru symbolizes as the crowned king of the two lands ⚚ (Upper and Lower Egypt) symbolizing the union of the lower and the Higher Self. The Winged Sundisk is the fullness of spiritual realization, the understanding and awareness of the all encompassing nature of the Divine Self which enfolds all within its wings as it were. It means transcending duality and discovering the non-duality of the Higher Self which encompasses the good and the bad.

May you and your child discover the glory of
Asar, Aset and Heru!

Other Books From C. M. Books P.O.Box 570459 Miami, Florida, 33257 (305) 378-6253 Fax: (305) 378-6253

This book is part of a series on the study and practice of Ancient Egyptian Yoga and Mystical Spirituality based on the writings of Dr. Muata Abhaya Ashby. They are also part of the Egyptian Yoga Course provided by the Sema Institute of Yoga. Below you will find a listing of the other books in this series. For more information send for the Egyptian Yoga Book-Audio-Video Catalog or the Egyptian Yoga Course Catalog.

INTRODUCTION
To
YOGA PHILOSOPHY
AND MYSTICAL RELIGION

**by
Dr. Muata Abhaya Ashby**

Now you can study the teachings of Egyptian and Indian Yoga wisdom and Spirituality with the Egyptian Yoga Mystical Spirituality Series. The Egyptian Yoga Series takes you through the Initiation process and lead you to understand the mysteries of the soul and the Divine and to attain the highest goal of life: ENLIGHTENMENT. The *Egyptian Yoga Series*, takes you on an in depth study of Ancient Egyptian mythology and their inner mystical meaning. Each Book is prepared for the serious student of the mystical sciences and provides a study of the teachings along with exercises, assignments and projects to make the teachings understood and effective in real life. The Series is part of the Egyptian Yoga course but may be purchased even if you are not taking the course. The series is ideal for study groups.
Prices subject to change.

NOTE: For more information on the *Egyptian Yoga Book Series* and the Egyptian Yoga Course of studies in religion and Yoga see the *Egyptian Yoga Guide.*

For those parents who are seriously interested in following the path of Shetaut Asar (Ausarian Resurrection Mystical Religion) it is strongly suggested that they study the books: *The Ausarian Resurrection: The Ancient Egyptian Bible* and *The Mystical Teachings of The Ausarian Resurrection: Initiation Into The Third Level of Shetaut Asar, Mysticism of Ushet Rekhat: Worship of the Divine Mother* and *The Wisdom of Maati: Spiritual Enlightenment Through The Path of Virtuous Living.*

THE AUSARIAN RESURRECTION:
The Ancient Egyptian Bible

The Ancient Sages created stories based on human and superhuman beings whose struggles, aspirations, needs and desires ultimately lead them to discover their true Self. The myth of Isis, Asar and Horus is no exception in this area. While there is no one source where the entire story may be found, pieces of it are inscribed in various ancient temples walls, tombs, steles and papyri. For the first time available, the complete myth of Asar, Isis and Horus has been compiled from original Ancient Egyptian, Greek and Coptic Texts. This epic myth has been richly illustrated with reliefs from the temple of Horus at Edfu, the temple of Isis at Philae, the temple of Asar at Abydos, the temple of Hathor at Denderah and various papyri, inscriptions and reliefs.

Discover the myth which inspired the teachings of the *Shetaut Neter* (Egyptian Mystery System - Egyptian Yoga) and the Egyptian Book of Coming Forth By Day. Also, discover the three levels of Ancient Egyptian Religion, how to understand the mysteries of the Tuat or Astral World and how to discover the abode of the Supreme in the Amenta, *The Other World*.

The ancient religion of Asar, Isis and Horus, if properly understood, contains all of the elements necessary to lead the sincere aspirant to attain immortality through inner self-discovery. This volume presents the entire myth and explores the main mystical themes and rituals associated with the myth for understating human existence, creation and the way to achieve spiritual emancipation - *Resurrection*. The Osirian myth is so powerful that it influenced and is still having an effect on the major world religions. Discover the origins and mystical meaning of the Christian Trinity, the Eucharist ritual and the ancient origin of the birthday of Jesus Christ. **191 Pages 8.5" X 11" Hard Cover ISBN: 1-884564-12-7 $29.99 U.S. Soft Cover ISBN: 1-884564-27-5 $18.95**

THE MYSTICAL TEACHINGS
OF
THE AUSARIAN RESURRECTION

This Volume will detail the myth of the Osirian Resurrection and The Story of Horus and Set and their mystical implications in the life of the aspirant/initiate. Then this volume will turn to a line by line mystical reading of the myth in order to uncover the mystical implications of the epic story. Mythology will come alive as a message from the Sages of ancient times to the initiates and not just as stories for entertainment. This Volume is special because it links the individual student to the myth and thereby gives her/him deep insight into his/her own true nature and how to practice the religion of Asar, Isis and Horus. This volume may be used as a companion to the book *The Ausarian Resurrection: The Ancient Egyptian Bible* by Muata Ashby (see the description above). **232 pages 5.5"x 8.5" ISBN: 1-884564-22-4 $15.99**

MYSTICISM OF USHET REKHAT:
Worship of the Divine Mother

The Supreme Being may be worshipped as father or as mother. *Ushet Rekhat* or *Mother Worship*, is the spiritual process of worshipping the Divine in the form of the Divine Goddess. It celebrates the most important forms of the Goddess including *Nathor, Maat, Aset, Arat, Amentet and Hathor* and explores their mystical meaning as well as the rising of *Sirius*, the star of Aset (Isis) and the new birth of Hor (Horus). The end of the year is a time of reckoning, reflection and engendering a new or renewed positive movement toward attaining spiritual enlightenment. The Mother Worship devotional meditation ritual, performed on five days during the month of December and on New Year's Eve, is based on the Ushet Rekhit. During the ceremony, the cosmic forces, symbolized by Sirius ✶ and the constellation of Orion ✶✶✶, are harnessed through the understanding and devotional attitude of the participant. This propitiation draws the light of wisdom and health to all those who share in the ritual, leading to prosperity and wisdom. **$9.95 - 5.5"x 8.5" ISBN 1-884564-18-6**

THE WISDOM OF MAATI:
Spiritual Enlightenment Through the Path of Virtue

Known as Karma Yoga in India, the teachings of MAAT for living virtuously and with orderly wisdom are explained and the student is to begin practicing the precepts of Maat in daily life so as to promote the process of purification of the heart in preparation for the judgment of the soul. This judgment will be understood not as an event that will occur at the time of death but as an event that occurs continuously, at every moment in the life of the individual. The student will learn how to become allied with the forces of the Higher Self and to thereby begin cleansing the mind (heart) of impurities so as to attain a higher vision of reality. **196 pages 5.5"x 8.5" ISBN 1-884564-20-8 $15.99**

EGYPTIAN YOGA:
THE PHILOSOPHY OF ENLIGHTENMENT

An original, fully illustrated work, including hieroglyphs, detailing the meaning of the Egyptian mysteries, tantric yoga, psycho-spiritual and physical exercises. Egyptian Yoga is a guide to the practice of the highest spiritual philosophy which leads to absolute freedom from human misery and to immortality. It is well known by scholars that Egyptian philosophy is the basis of Western and Middle Eastern religious philosophies such as *Christianity, Islam, Judaism,* the *Kabbalah,* and Greek philosophy, but what about Indian philosophy, Yoga and Taoism? What were the original teachings? How can they be practiced today? What is the source of pain and suffering in the world and what is the solution? Discover the deepest mysteries of the mind and universe within and outside of your self. **216 Pages 8.5" X 11" ISBN: 1-884564-01-1 Soft $18.95 U.S.**

INITIATION INTO EGYPTIAN YOGA:
The Secrets of Sheti

Sheti: Spiritual discipline or program, to go deeply into the mysteries, to study the mystery teachings and literature profoundly, to penetrate the mysteries.

? You will learn about the mysteries of initiation into the teachings and practice of Yoga and how to become an Initiate of the mystical sciences.

This insightful manual is the first in a series which introduces you to the goals of daily spiritual and yoga practices: Meditation, Diet, Words of Power and the ancient wisdom teachings. **150 pages 8.5" X 11" ISBN 1-884564-02-X   Soft Cover $16.99 U.S.**

EGYPTIAN PROVERBS:
TEMT TCHAAS

Temt Tchaas means: collection of Ancient Egyptian Proverbs
   ? How to live according to MAAT Philosophy.
   ? Beginning Meditation.
   ? All proverbs are indexed for easy searches.
For the first time in one volume, Ancient Egyptian proverbs, wisdom teachings and meditations, fully illustrated with hieroglyphic text and symbols. EGYPTIAN PROVERBS is a unique collection of knowledge and wisdom which you can put into practice today and transform your life. **160 pages. 5.5"x 8.5" $9.95 U.S ISBN: 1-884564-00-3**

EGYPTIAN YOGA EXERCISE
WORKOUT BOOK
Thef Neteru:
The Movement of The Gods and Goddesses

Discover the physical postures and exercises practiced thousands of years ago in Ancient Egypt which are today known as Yoga exercises. This work is based on the pictures and teachings from the Creation story of Ra, The Osirian Resurrection Myth and the carvings and reliefs from various Temples in Ancient Egypt. **130 Pages 8.5" X 11" ISBN 1-884564-10-0 Soft Cover $16.99 Exercise video $19.99**

THE CYCLES OF TIME:
The Ancient Origins of Yoga in Egypt and India

This Volume will cover the ancient origins of Yoga and establish a link between the cultures of Ancient Egypt and ancient and modern India. This Volume is of paramount importance because it shows that Egyptian Philosophy began over 30,000 years ago and did not die out along with Egyptian society but that it was carried on by the Sages and Saints who left Egypt at the time of its social collapse. **200 pages. 5.5"x 8.5" ISBN 1-884564-13-5 $14.99**

THE HIDDEN PROPERTIES OF MATTER:
Egyptian Physics and
Yoga Metaphysics.

This Volume will go deeper into the philosophy of God as creation and will explore the concepts of modern science and how they correlate with ancient teachings. This Volume will lay the ground work for the understanding of the philosophy of universal consciousness and the initiatic/yogic insight into who or what is God? **175 pages. 5.5"x 8.5" ISBN 1-884564-07-0 $14.99**

THE WISDOM OF ISIS: GOD IN THE UNIVERSE, GOD IN THE HEART
Who is God in the light of
Yoga Philosophy?

Through the study of ancient myth and the illumination of initiatic understanding the idea of God is expanded from the mythological comprehension to the metaphysical. Then this metaphysical understanding is related to you, the student, so as to begin understanding your true divine nature. **5.5"x 8.5" ISBN 1-884564-24-0 $15.99**

EGYPTIAN TANTRA YOGA:
The Art of Sex Sublimation

This Volume will expand on the male and female principles within the human body and in the universe and further detail the sublimation of sexual energy into spiritual energy. The student will study the deities Min and Hathor, Asar and Isis, Geb and Nut and discover the mystical implications for a practical spiritual discipline. This Volume will also focus on the Tantric aspects of Ancient Egyptian and Indian mysticism, the purpose of sex and the mystical teachings of sexual sublimation which lead to self-knowledge and enlightenment. **196 pages 5.5"x 8.5" ISBN 1-884564-03-8** $15.99

MEDITATION
The Ancient Egyptian Path to Enlightenment

Many people do not know about the rich history of meditation practice in Ancient Egypt. This volume outlines the theory of meditation and presents the Ancient Egyptian Hieroglyphic text which give instruction as to the nature of the mind and its three modes of expression. It also presents the texts which give instruction on the practice of meditation for spiritual enlightenment and unity with the Divine. This volume allows the reader to begin practicing meditation by explaining, in easy to understand terms, the simplest form of meditation and working up to the most advanced form which was practiced in ancient times and which is still practiced by yogis around the world in modern times. **260 pages 5.5"x 8.5" ISBN 1-884564-27-7 $16.99**

HEALING THE CRIMINAL HEART
Introduction to Maat Philosophy, Yoga and Spiritual Redemption Through the Path of Virtue

Who is a criminal? Is there such a thing as a criminal heart? What is the source of evil and sinfulness and is there any way to rise above it? Is there redemption for those who have committed sins, even the worst crimes?

Ancient Egyptian mystical psychology holds important answers to these questions. Over ten thousand years ago mystical psychologists, the Sages of Ancient Egypt, studied and charted the human mind and spirit and laid out a path which will lead to spiritual redemption, prosperity and enlightenment.

This introductory volume brings forth the teachings of the Ausarian Resurrection, the most important myth of Ancient Egypt, with relation to the faults of human existence: anger, hatred, greed, lust, animosity, discontent, ignorance, egoism jealousy, bitterness, and a myriad of psycho-spiritual ailments which keep a human being in a state of negativity and adversity.
40 pages 5.5"x 8.5" ISBN: 1-884564-17-8 $3.99

INTRODUCTION TO YOGA AND MYSTICAL RELIGION

The Egyptian Yoga Guide is a comprehensive pamphlet which helps you to navigate through the Egyptian Yoga Book Series as well as the program of yoga and or religious studies based on the book series. The Egyptian Yoga Guide assists you in understanding the meaning and purpose of Egyptian Yoga by introducing the main concepts and goals. Then the guide helps you to determining what kind of personality you have and what form of spiritual study and practice is best suited for you. Then the guide helps you to understand the process of spiritual evolution and the way to promote spiritual knowledge. The guide is free with your purchase of any book in the Egyptian Yoga Book Series. Simply request one with your order. 20 **pages 5.5"x 8.5" ISBN: 1-884564-29-1 $4.95**